nF419405

# Daisy Doo
## All the Sounds She Knew

Written by Daisy Kent

Illustrated by Maryna Kovinka

Daisy Doo: All the Sounds She Knew

Copyright © 2023 by Daisy Kent.
All rights reserved.

ISBN 979-8-9888517-0-7
ISBN 979-8-9888517-1-4

Dedicated to
Dr. Kari and the medical staff at UCSD, 

Thank you for helping a little girl see
how beautiful her life would be.

  To every little girl,

What makes you unique makes you beautiful.
Let your light shine.

Daisy Doo was a silly little boo!
She would play all day and eat chocolate fondue!

She loved to sing, and drum, and have lots of fun!
She flipped, and dipped, and could do the splits!

Daisy Doo loved the sound when the rain drizzled.

The big loud BOOM

as the fireworks sizzled!

And when her goofy best friend shouted...

"I LOVE PICKLES!"

The birds sang lullabies when they chirped...

and she giggled and giggled when her brother would

BURP!

Daisy Doo heard lions ROAR...
and jumped at the slam of a door!

Then one day, little Daisy Doo grew...
      and her life went into a big... HUGE spew!
She could only hear half of her mother's silly laugh.

Her hair was frizzy, and she started getting dizzy!

Her ears popped, and her heart dropped!

Daisy Doo could no longer hear the rain drizzle,
the fireworks sizzle, or her best friend shouting,
"I LOVE PICKLES!"
Birds didn't chirp, and her brother didn't burp!
She couldn't hear the lions roar or the slam of the door!

Daisy Doo began to fear
because she could no longer hear!

Daisy Doo met Dr. Kari! Who said,
"Don't you be sorry!

It is okay to feel blue, but there are things we can do!
I know a trick that will help you quite a bit!"

Daisy Doo had to have surgery,
and she did feel a bit of worry.
She cried and would hide, and had deep feelings inside.

But Dr. Kari was smart and had a good heart!
She wanted the best for little Daisy Doo.

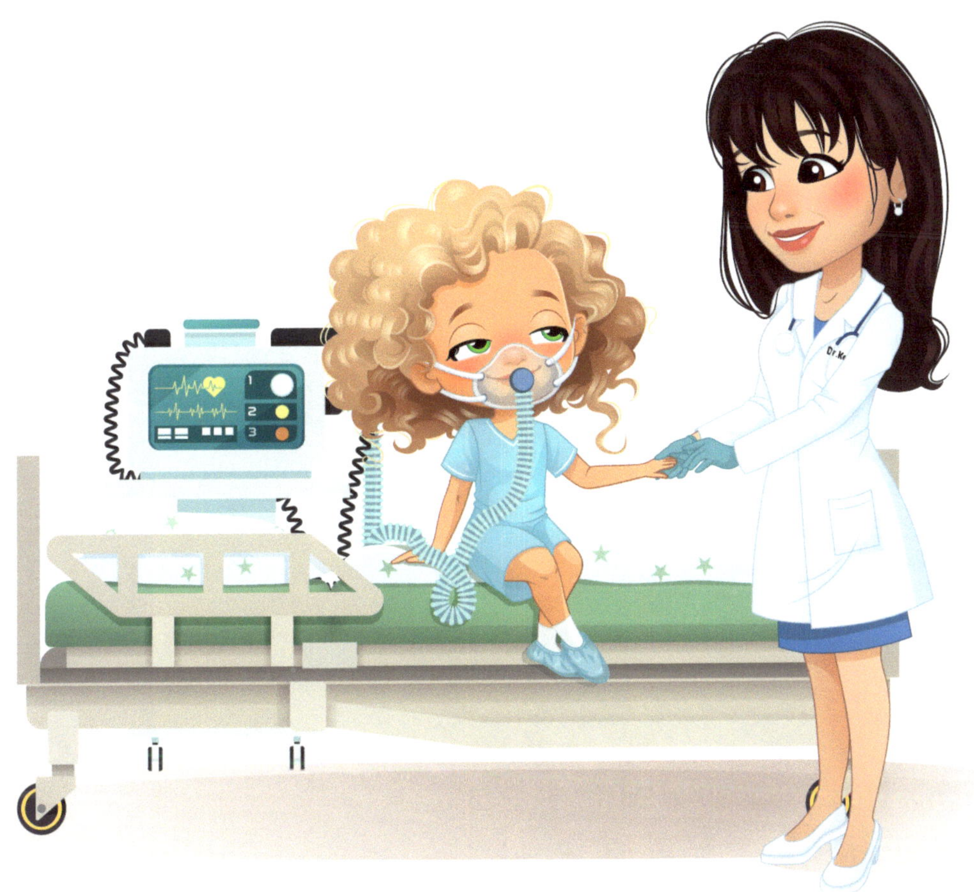

So, to sleep went little Daisy Doo...
and she got a device that would help her very nicely!

A cochlear implant was now part of Daisy Doo!
She had a little bit of pain, but a lot to gain!

Daisy Doo had to practice...
                    but then...

Her cochlear implant became fantastic!
To her surprise, when she opened her eyes...
Daisy Doo began to see how happy she was to be!

Daisy Doo could now hear the rain drizzle,
the fireworks sizzle, and her best friend shout,
"I LOVE PICKLES!"
The lions roared, and she could hear the slam of a door!

Daisy Doo, well... what did she do?
She grew more and more and had fun once more!

Her world came alive!
She hears bees buzz in the hive!

The bark of a dog!
The ribbit of a frog!

Her mother's laugh is no
longer just half!

The big cannon ball splash!
The waves crash!

She sings, and drums, and has lots of fun!
She flips, and dips, and does the splits!

Daisy Doo now knew this was
the best thing she ever did do!
Little Daisy Doo is the happiest big boo!

And guess what?

Daisy Doo still eats chocolate fondue!

Mom and Dad,

Thank you for showing me
the beauty in life's unexpected moments.


All my love, Daisy.

www.ingramcontent.com/pod-product-compliance
Lightning Source LLC
Chambersburg PA
CBHW042026110726
48010CB00007B/245